The Kingdom Within

Torn Curtain Publishing
Wellington, New Zealand
www.torncurtainpublishing.com

© Copyright 2022 Sharon Reynolds. All rights reserved.

ISBN Softcover 978-0-473-64769-8

No portion of this book may be reproduced, stored in a retrieval system or transmitted in any form or by any means—electronic, mechanical, photocopy, recording or otherwise—except for brief quotations in printed reviews or promotion, without prior written permission from the author.

Unless otherwise noted, all scripture is taken from the New King James Version. Copyright © 1982 by Thomas Nelson, Inc. Used by permission. All rights reserved.

Scripture quotations marked (NIV) are taken from the Holy Bible, New International Version®, NIV®. Copyright © 1973, 1978, 1984, 2011 by Biblica, Inc.™ Used by permission of Zondervan. All rights reserved worldwide. www.zondervan.com

Scripture marked NCV are taken from the New Century Version®. Copyright © 2005 by Thomas Nelson. Used by permission. All rights reserved.

Scripture quotations marked ESV are from The Holy Bible, English Standard Version®, copyright © 2001 by Crossway, a publishing ministry of Good News Publishers. Used by permission. All rights reserved.

Scriptures marked ERV are taken from the Holy Bible: Easy-to-Read Version (ERV), International Edition © 2013, 2016 by Bible League International. Used by permission.

Cover photography by Tatiana Gluhova. Used with permission.
Typeset in Palatino, Baskerville and Connoisseurs

Cataloging in Publishing Data
  Title: The Kingdom Within
  Author: Sharon Reynolds
  Subjects: Christian living, Spiritual growth, Women's interests, Self help.

A copy of this title is held in the National Library of New Zealand

Sharon Reynold's *The Kingdom Within* is a beautiful story of transformation. She writes with transparency how she allowed the Holy Spirit to heal the deepest hurts and places of the heart and shares great truths which were revealed to help those who have carried pain for many years and never knew how to access the deeper places of the heart. There is hope when all seems hopeless, there is joy that comes in the morning. I highly recommend you read this book. Get ready for your own heart to relate as you read Sharon's process of discovering her true identity, her inheritance in Christ, and the Kingdom Within, which brought her tremendous freedom.

Jennifer Eivaz
Co-Pastor, Harvest Church
Founder, Harvest Ministries International

Turlock California, United States of America *The Kingdom Within* brings to light how the Kingdom of Heaven is truly inside every believer, but to access it we must be willing to tear down the false kingdoms we have built along our journey in life. I love how Sharon's book doesn't just explain how to access the 'Kingdom Within'; she has written it in a way that will spark deeper thought and revelation in the reader. This revelation will take you on a personal pilgrimage with Holy Spirit to unlock the purpose and plans He placed in you before He placed you in your mother's womb, and expose what is in the way of you taking hold of the Kingdom dominion we have been granted access to.

Sharon reminds us that it takes faith, courage and tenacity to go after whatever is in the way of the promise, and that our willingness to grab hold of it will unlock doors not only for ourselves and our families, but that generations to come will also reap the reward. This book speaks about justice for the believer, our rights as a kingdom citizen, and the inheritance God has for us as sons and daughters of the King. It will take you on an expedition of the heart and give you an invitation to exchange what you've built for what God has designed.

Prophetess Michelle Farrar
Inner Healing and Deliverance Minister, Life Coach
United States of America

This new book by Sharon, is as raw as she is. Each chapter is full of revelation and challenges us to deal with the limitations that keep us from entering into the fullness of the Kingdom of God within us. As we deal with pain, trauma and unforgiveness, we are able to enter into that fullness. Sharon's book will lead you to experience a new level of love, and to enter realms of God's Glory that most people have never experienced.

Ps. Luis Gonzalez
Endorsed Minister & Pastor
The Master's House Church, Taree, Australia

So many people long for mentors to show them how to walk successfully in the ways of the Spirit. As evident from her book, Sharon is a woman who has walked out the word before she has written about it. The words you are about to receive will bring you to a place of unshakable faith as Sharon takes you on an amazing journey through the Word and her encounters with the Word to being an overcomer. As you read, Sharon will impart the keys God gave her. These will equip you too, in overcoming whatever area you are facing on your journey of restoration. You will marvel as Sharon shares her experiences of redemption as a woman who draws into the Father's love for every situation. I couldn't put the book down.

Nellie O'Hara
Author. Speaker & Mentor
Christian Services Association, Canada

Sharon Reynold's book, *The Kingdom Within*, invites you into her journey of finding hope and joy in the midst of pain and suffering. Sharon shares how God taught her to exchange grief and disappointment for true heart restoration as a daughter of the King. This book will encourage you to walk in the resurrection power that God has provided to transform firstly your own life, and then the lives of those around you as you apply the principles Sharon teaches you.

Wendy Peter
Ministry Director
Women on the Frontlines (WOFL) Global

The Kingdom Within

SHARON REYNOLDS

This book is dedicated with thanks to God.
My story only exists because of Him.
Without God, there would be no story at all,

and

to my incredible family, who sacrifice constantly
for the birthing of new things.

TO THE READER

It is my earnest prayer that you will encounter the Spirit of God in such a way that you are not the same when you reach the end of the book as when you began. I pray a blessing over you, and over the story God is writing in your life today.
—Sharon Reynolds

CONTENTS

Introduction		1
PART ONE:	**RESURRECTION JOY**	
Chapter 1	Pain and Suffering	9
Chapter 2	Justice and Glory	13
Chapter 3	Exchange of Joy	19
Chapter 4	Heart Restoration	25
Chapter 5	Strong Hearts	30
PART TWO:	**RESURRECTION POWER**	
Chapter 6	Afflicted	37
Chapter 7	Overcomers	41
Chapter 8	Inheritance	45
Chapter 9	Seeing and Knowing	48
Chapter 10	Ministering in Faith	53
Chapter 11	God's Daughters	57

PART THREE: RESURRECTION LIFE

Chapter 12   A Little Oil 65

Chapter 13   Full Inheritance .71

Chapter 14   Promised Land .79

Chapter 15   Garments of Majesty 85

An Invitation 95

Declaration 97

Prophetic Word for the Author 99

Acknowledgments 101

About the Author 103

INTRODUCTION

"Looking unto Jesus, the author and finisher of our faith, who for the joy that was set before Him endured the cross, despising the shame, and has sat down at the right hand of the throne of God."
Hebrews 12:2

This book is full of truths whose mission is to infuse hope within you, along with a sense that you as His sons and daughters are more than able to accomplish the dreams He puts in your heart, for in Him all things are possible.

The stories you are about to read are true accounts from God's Word of the lives of conquerors and overcomers, interwoven with reflections from my own journals. Do you seek the power to overcome in your own life? If so, I trust that the same God who met with me will also meet with you, exactly where you are at right now.

The Kingdom Within is the understanding that we, as sons and daughters of God, carry the kingdom inside of us. We are royalty! We display God's manifest glory here on earth. God's glory is more than splendor, or radiance.

Its essence is love. We have been called and created for love, by Love Himself. This gives us power to partner with God. From an overflow of love, we administer the kingdom of God Almighty, the creator of all. Once we know who we are as sons and daughters of the King, we can begin to live powerfully from the heart, assured of His promises.

Many of us, however, have experienced heartbreak. This is my story too. But as I overcame the obstacles my heart had erected over years of pain, wounds, and hidden trauma, this truth became evident: The kingdom is within!

As I pursued this truth, Holy Spirit began to show me that our hearts are in fact an entire kingdom, a habitation of God's love. There was a greater love in my heart than I had realized.

As born-again believers, the Kingdom of God dwells within us. In the words of Galatians 2:20,

> "It is no longer I who live, but Christ lives in me."

The Kingdom of Heaven is not far away at all. It is near—in fact, it is within each one of us already. Our hearts house the Glory of God! When we discover this, we begin to encounter the same peace, joy, love and freedom that exists in heaven itself. But first, a restoration process is needed. After all, our hearts have been wounded. We need to rebuild God's Kingdom Within.

Let me share with you my personal discovery of the Glory of God manifesting within me. This revelation brought healing, and as I tell my story, I hope you also find healing for your heart.

INTRODUCTION

All I ever wanted was to be loved. My entire life I have sought love. From the moment I took my first breath love has been my pursuit, and it will be until the day I breathe my last.

It's not that I never knew love growing up, never saw, tasted, or experienced love. I did, but I had a driving force within me to find *a deeper* love. I had an insatiable desire for more than the superficial human love that, over the years, had come and gone in my life. Human love is nothing in comparison to God's all-encompassing, magnificent love. I was on a journey after something more. More than I knew already. There was a gnawing hunger within my soul that was just not satisfied with the love I had already experienced in my life. Internally, I just knew there was more to be had.

As I pursued this great capacity and longing for love in my heart, Holy Spirit began to lead me and show me more of the Kingdom of God that dwells within us. He began by speaking to me about my heart and the 'Kingdom Within'.

> *"The Lord is close to the brokenhearted and saves those*
> *who are crushed in spirit."*
> Psalm 34:18 (NIV)

At the age of forty-eight, my father unexpectedly passed away. In that moment, my entire world was turned upside down. The grief of his sudden loss and the truths it exposed, left me crushed and hanging by a thread emotionally as my heart broke into a million pieces of pain. I was the apple of my father's eye. I loved him deeply, and his death came as a total shock.

My husband and I had only just landed in our beloved Papua New Guinea where we were about to embark on a season of ministry. Our previous time in Papua New Guinea had also been cut short—now, with the news of my father's death, we had once again 'been exited'. I felt cheated and robbed, yet again. Papua New Guinea had become a 'heart place' for me, and we had worked so hard to return, yet here we were leaving. We had no choice, we had to go, but we felt deeply that we had not finished what we came for.

My father would not have cared if I had returned home or stayed in Papua New Guinea. I knew he would have been happy for me to continue delivering the message he had come to know was inside me. However, Papua New Guinean culture places a high priority on honoring parents, especially fathers, both in life and in death. As much as I wanted to fulfill God's call to minister at the events that had been planned and to honor the sacrifices of those who had prepared faithfully for the spiritual harvest awaiting us, we just could not.

My heart felt crushed at both the loss of my father and having to leave Papua New Guinea behind. In the hours of my initial grief, Holy Spirit counseled me gently and wisely. He showed me that the greater witness of God's love was to honor my father in his death, and assured me that returning home to New Zealand would speak louder than anything else in that moment.

The flights home to New Zealand to farewell my father seemed so long. I arrived exhausted but felt prepared to say goodbye. By God's grace, I arrived and was able to speak at my father's funeral. There was favor on my words as I gave the eulogy. I spoke of the wonderful man that, in my eyes, my father had been. We had our differences while I was growing up, as most fathers and daughters do, but I knew without a doubt that he loved me. It was only after the funeral, when I returned home, that I received the news that the man I had just farewelled was, in fact, not my biological father.

This was a complete shock. I had already been through such a process to understand my identity, and this news rocked my world entirely. For forty-eight years, I had believed I was all the things my bloodline supposedly said of me. Now, I had no idea what was true. It was a blow from the enemy designed to take me out completely—and for a while, it certainly did.

Over the next two years, however, Holy Spirit walked so closely with me as I grieved and tried to make sense of the pain my 'father's' death and the subsequent news had caused in my heart. My heart pain was so strong and overwhelming at times I wasn't sure I would make it. Yet, I knew that I had already come too far to let pain and bitterness rule my life, so I pressed into Holy Spirit and, like the woman in Luke 8, held tight to the hem of the garment of Jesus.

What began as a shock became a time of great healing and restoration as I found my true identity in my heavenly Father and the inheritance I have in Him. Over time, I began to recover from the losses of my earthly identity and the father I had come to love, and found new strength and courage.

It was as He took me deep within my own heart that He revealed the truth of the hidden 'Kingdom Within'. My heart had become a kingdom of woundedness and pain. My subconscious response was to fill it with human love. But as the healing process began, He showed me how to build a secure kingdom, a Kingdom of Glory.

Tearing down the vulnerable foundations to lay a lasting foundation of love was something I could never do alone. I needed Holy Spirit's revelation, and the encouragement of others. That is why I have written this book. I want you to know that as you begin the difficult but lasting process of rebuilding the *Kingdom Within*, you are not alone. This is your time of redemptive glory. There is hope!

This book contains a simple yet deep revelation from the Spirit of God. My prayer is that as the *Kingdom Within* is rebuilt piece by piece, you too will experience full restoration and become a carrier of all He intended for you. We are new creations in Christ (2 Corinthians 5:17). Once we were lost and far off, and then we came near. When we return to God, we are adopted by His Spirit and are now sons and daughters! From that moment, our lives are transformed. This is salvation, and it is a free gift. Sanctification, however, is a process which some have described as the 'cleaning-up' period of our hearts and all that has troubled them until that salvation moment. Even after salvation, we often have dark areas we still need to partner with Holy Spirit to clean out. Sometimes people speak of this as 'inner healing' or 'deliverance'. You will find prayers at the end of some chapters to help you engage with Holy Spirit for your own healing and deliverance.

This book is the account of my own unique encounter with the Spirit of God as He revealed that the *Kingdom Within* was my own heart. It had layers of woundedness, yet He came to restore my heart and give it a new identity as one who is filled with God's glory. As Holy Spirit reveals the truth of your own heart, may you also experience transformation and become a conduit of His Glory.

We are a manifestation of heaven on earth!

PART ONE

RESURRECTION JOY

1

PAIN AND SUFFERING

*"O Lord, You are the portion of my inheritance and my cup;
You maintain my lot. The lines have fallen to me in pleasant places;
Yes, I have a good inheritance."*
Psalm 16:5-6

I sat with my eyes shut, listening to worship music. In the spirit, I saw a pencil emerge and start writing. I noticed it was rewriting over the pages of a story that had already been written. The pencil seemed to be in my hand, but it was not really me that was doing the writing. Then I heard the words, *He's writing a new story.*

I continued to watch as the pencil moved freely over the paper when another thought arrived: *I am not the author. God is the author, yet the story is in my hands.*

That's when I understood that God was writing over the story I had already written for my life. In that moment, it was as if years of hurt and pain were being supernaturally erased, and a hope-filled future emerged.

Pain and suffering have a way of editing the good plans and purposes God laid in our hearts from the beginning. Yet in my vision, He was rewriting over the pain, restoring His original design for me, and revealing the truth of who I am in Christ—His beloved daughter. What had been written before was disappearing right now before my very eyes. On the page in front of me, new words were being laid down for me to take hold of.

This was grace in the making. He had, in one act, healed my pain and realigned my life with the story He had purposed all along.

The scriptures tell us that God sanctifies us (or 'washes us clean') through His Word (Ephesians 5:26). That was my reality. His words on the page in my vision cleansed my heart from the sorrow and grief I had built my life upon. It was as if the words formed by my heavenly Father's hand had been written directly onto my heart. Until that point, I had been the author of my inner life. Now it was time for me to allow God, the true Author, to write the story of my 'Kingdom Within'.

His words of life not only washed my tainted story clean—they became a lamp to my feet (Psalm 119:105). As I took tentative steps forward, I found light on my pathway. It was as if all that He had promised me in previous times of hardship was now possible. Old expectations disappeared as confidence and joy emerged.

"Looking unto Jesus, the author and finisher of our faith, who for the joy that was set before Him endured the cross, despising the shame, and has sat down at the right hand of the throne of God."
Hebrews 12:2

Now I had a new identity, new clarity for the path ahead. But there was more on the page God had written, and it brought powerful healing to my heart.

God had written a new inheritance for me! Where all that was mine had previously been unknown or denied to me, I now had promises to lay hold of. I began thanking God for the delivery of my true and full inheritance in Him. In my heart, I could already see the glory God had designed for me to possess. I began declaring:

"I will walk in the fullness of His promises as a daughter of God! All power and authority that is given to me will begin to manifest as God's favor and glory in my life. I will live and walk in resurrection power and nothing less from here on in. No scheme of man shall enter my mind, body or spirit. I am holy ground. Amen!"

As a Seer-prophet, God speaks to me primarily in creative and visual language. I often 'see' things very differently from others. Sometimes, when I read my Bible, the words literally jump up from the pages and spring to life in front of me.

We all have a unique way of communicating with God, and He with us. As Holy Spirit began speaking through His living word to me, He emphasized the need to 'cross over' into my inheritance. What this meant would unfold over time. But for now, I was on a journey of deep heart healing. God had further truth to unravel to my heart, a revelation of the circumstances that led to my birth.

The truth that came out after my father's funeral had shocked me to the core. Later, however, I found out something I had never known in my growing-up years—that my 'father' had deliberately made a choice to become my father even before I was born. That realization brought resolution to my pain. But it was a supernatural encounter with God that brought lasting transformation.

The truth about my earthly father became a springboard for God to show me His redemptive plan for my life. Even before I was born, God had chosen an earthly father for me who would love me just as He did, unconditionally and deeply. How wonderful!

In a beautiful picture, God showed me He had prepared a place for me at His table. As I healed, I saw others like me gathering in the secret place with Him, a place where He reveals strategies and plans to deliver each of us from the depths of our heart-crushing pain. As I received that awareness, the broken part of my heart began to be resurrected. I was being brought back from death to life. I knew I was loved with an everlasting love. Nothing could separate me from the love of God! Immersed in God's great love, I was able to reconcile my pain and be even more thankful for my earthly father, knowing he had sacrificed so much to make me his child.

We all search for significance in our own way. Some people join gangs, looking for acceptance, belonging and identity. Others join churches for the same reasons. But ultimately, our identity and belonging are in Christ. He lives in us (Galatians 2:20, Colossians 1:27), and we are in Him (2 Corinthians 5:17, Colossians 2:10).

2

JUSTICE AND GLORY

"You changed my sorrow into dancing, you took away my clothes of sadness, and clothed me in happiness. I will sing to you and not be silent Lord, my God, I will praise you forever."
Psalm 30:11-12 (NCV)

God had caused me to turn towards myself and look inside my own heart, to discover *my* 'Kingdom Within'. What I found, was that my heart craved something more than love and acceptance. In my heart of hearts was a cry for justice. The more healing I received, the more I wanted justice for all the pain and suffering I had endured. I felt it was owed to me. I wanted restitution for the years of ill treatment, vindication for injustices committed against me. I carried scars from my childhood right into adulthood, and the Kingdom within me sought justice for all the wrongs and trauma they represented.

Years of being misunderstood and devalued by people who should have provided protection, nurture and encouragement had resulted in layers of pain that had hardened my heart. Bitterness and betrayal had formed strongholds inside my heart. I had created a hostile gatekeeper for my own heart who was seeking justice at every turn, craving restitution for all the wrongs that afflicted my soul.

Now, Holy Spirit was showing me that my constant need for justice to be done was holding me bound. Yet all the while, He was here to set the captive—my heart—free!

He began to show me that He was my vindicator.

He would do what I could never do for myself.

That day I saw the picture of the place He prepared for me at His table, God began to deliver me into freedom from the oppression I had been suffering for so long from the gatekeeper of my own heart.

The following morning, Holy Spirit instructed me to look up the word 'justice' in the Oxford Dictionary. This is what I read:

Justice; noun

1. Just behavior or treatment – the quality of being just

2. The administration of law or authority in maintaining this

3. A judge or magistrate.

The original word 'justice' comes from the Latin word *justus*, meaning 'morally right and fair'. The Bible often uses the word 'righteous' in a similar way. I had never considered that before. Were justice and righteousness inseparably linked?

As I studied further, I discovered that indeed, 'justice' and 'righteousness' are powerfully connected. However, justice does not always look the way we think it should, and how it is achieved is completely up to God.

The kingdom within our hearts holds many things, and one thing my kingdom had been built upon was an inert sense of justice. Wherever there was pain, suffering, or oppression of any sort, I was ready to battle. I had been like that all my life. Yet my heart was experiencing deep injustice, and as I cried out to God for healing, He began to shift my understanding and bring His truth to the situation.

What I discovered is that God's justice is not our idea of justice, or certainly it was not my idea of what I thought justice meant. I had a lot to learn. I seemed continuously drawn towards situations where it was as if a switch would go on inside of me. I would 'power up' whenever a worthy cause came my way.

It was as if I was internally wired to just fight against anything I perceived to be oppressive. I realized that even as a small child I had shown these tendencies. Growing up, my father had often commented on it, describing me as the 'Protector of the downtrodden'.

However, in my search for deeper understanding of this trait, I found that my passion for what I thought was justice was really a deep need to stand up against *injustice*.

The two are not the same.

In Deuteronomy 32, God takes Moses up the mountain to show him the 'Promised Land' before he dies. God had asked Moses to lead His people to possess this land. Then, in what appears to be a moment of God going back on His promise, God says Moses will not enter the land after all. For some reason, God is showing him what he will *not* experience, all the while assuring him that He is keeping His promise.

It may seem a little cruel to us that God would show Moses the Promised Land and then not let him enter in. After an extremely dramatic escape from their oppressive tyrannical ruler, followed by roaming for forty years in the wilderness, the next generation will now finally get to the land God had promised.

But not Moses.

It's like showing a child a lollipop but telling them they can't lick it. They see it but don't get to experience it. Being so close you can taste it but knowing you will never have it seems incredibly mean and tormenting.

Why would God do something that looks so mean on the surface of it? Surely that's not justice for a man who gave up everything to obey God and deliver an entire nation of people from slavery?

This is where God's righteousness intersects with our sense of justice. Along the way, God had instructed both Moses and Aaron about how to meet the people's needs and relieve their burgeoning whining. "Speak to the rock," God had said. Instead, Moses struck the rock with his staff.

The message is simple: An unrighteous life will have consequences, naturally and eternally. Water still poured out from a rock in the driest of places, and God's people experienced provision. But Moses and his brother

Aaron dishonored God by not following God's instructions completely.

The truth is, God is not to be trifled with, nor will He take second place to anyone—even those He chooses and anoints. Moses and Aaron had not given Him the place of holiness, reverence, honor or respect He so deserved, and still requires from us today.

> *"I am the LORD; I have called you in righteousness; I will take you by the hand and keep you; I will give you as a covenant for the people, a light for the nations."*
> Isaiah 42:6 (ESV)

As I reflected on this verse, one phrase stood out to me: "I will take you by the hand and keep you." God was weaving another layer of robes around me. He loves justice and He honors the righteous. This promise brought vindication to my heart.

'Christ in us' means we too have been made right with God. As sons and daughters, we share His righteousness and become co-heirs, not of an earthly promise, but of the greatest inheritance ever given. We are the beneficiaries of His great love.

As we look at the injustices we have encountered through life, let us remember that God is a God who loves righteousness and acts justly. God's justice in the final days of Moses was that he saw the place of God's promise for the nation even though he himself would not enter it.

God is in the business of redeeming His people! Along the way, let us be careful to not leave Him out of the equation. He is to be honored and praised, for He is holy. God is in charge. We can bring to Him our need for justice for the wrongs we have endured, and look to Him to relieve the hurt that afflicts our soul.

As in the time of Moses, He is the provider, the holder of all power, and the One who brings us into the future He has promised for us. Psalm 37:6 says: "He shall bring forth your righteousness as the light, and your justice as the noonday."

Our job is to honor Him and give Him all the glory.

Prayer: Holy Spirit, I thank you that you bring forth my righteousness in the same way that you bring the light of day anew each morning. Thank you that your justice will prevail in my life. In Jesus' name, Amen.

3

EXCHANGE OF JOY

"You have made known to me the ways of life; You will make me full of joy in Your presence."
Acts 2:28

As I discovered God's heart for justice, I experienced an unexpected gift—the outpouring of joy. This makes sense. Often when joy is mentioned in the Bible, it is in relation to a wonderful exchange.

"You changed my sorrow into dancing, you took away my clothes of sadness, and clothed me in happiness."
Psalm 30:11 (NCV)

We can give our pain to God, knowing there is nothing He cannot redeem. As we trade our grievances for His righteousness, our hearts can begin to sing again. We can live with joy! Indeed, there is:

> *"... beauty for ashes, the oil of joy for mourning and the garment of praise for the spirit of heaviness."*
> Isaiah 61:3

What a transformation! As we give Him the sorrow and heaviness of our hearts, He in turn gives us beauty and happiness, dancing and joy. This is the anointing of God for those who overcome through His righteousness. Sorrow makes us weak, but the joy of the Lord is our place of strength. This is resurrection power!

In Luke 8:43-48 we read of a woman with an issue of blood who reached for Jesus' garment in desperation to receive healing in place of her affliction. I too sought the Lord, knowing that if I could only touch the hem of His love, I would be saved. In that moment, as I exchanged my need for justice with trust that God would vindicate me, the war in my heart was stilled.

The scripture says:

> *"The Lord your God in your midst, the Mighty One, will save; He will rejoice over you with gladness, He will quiet you with His love."*
> Zephaniah 3:17

This was my experience. God's Spirit, dwelling in my heart, replaced turmoil with rest.

One evening as I sat contemplating my journey into the joy of the Lord, Holy Spirit showed me that my desire for justice was not wrong—I had simply allowed it to steal my joy, but He had come to make it right. He is a restorer of justice *and* joy!

God was stripping away the injustices of my life, tearing down my inner walls, helping me work through deeply held griefs, and now bringing me to a place where I could receive justice. As I saw justice manifest in my life, my joy increased even more. God had brought me to a place of crossing over into joy!

As I grew in the knowledge of God's plan for joy in my life, I became increasingly aware of His plans for more restoration. His resurrection power was planning to accomplish the complete, supernatural healing of my heart.

One morning as I woke, I heard a proclamation from somewhere within me: "The walls of defense are coming down today!"

I sat bolt upright in my bed and looked around. *Who on earth could be saying that?* The words were so clear; there had to be someone in the room with me, surely! Of course, there was no one there but me. Well . . . me and Holy Spirit that is.

I was battling some old wounds and working them out with my good friend, Holy Spirit. My heart had begun to experience more freedom and light, but I had come to a point where I just felt stuck. I couldn't seem to get any further. It was like one of those 'mud runs'—the going is slow and sluggish because of the sheer thickness of the mud. The participants have a goal. They are focused and determined to wade through no matter how hard or how long. They have got to finish the race, but it is agonizingly slow to watch.

The process of healing the *Kingdom Within* can be a bit like this at times. Hurts build up and emotions get bogged down all at the same time, making getting in or out a difficult task for even the most mature of us. Feeling defeated yet again, I sat with the Lord that day and He began to show me the inside of my heart where I had built little kingdoms and then erected elaborate structures of defense to protect those kingdoms. My heart had experienced so much deliverance already, but there was still more to wade through.

As I persued the healing of my heart, I felt like one of these mud run participants. *Would the end ever be in sight?*

My friend, I tell you that scriptwriters could not come up with what I was about to experience. I was about to embark on an internal journey of epic proportions. It began when God gave me one word: *Blockages.*

Right then, I began to experience a very strange swelling in my abdomen. It was as if the blockages inside my heart started manifesting in the oddest way in my body. I sought medical advice, and after a myriad of tests, scans, and internal procedures, was told there was nothing wrong.

Knowing this was a spiritual matter, I submitted completely to a weekend of Holy Spirit encounter that I had already felt coming. I knew this time was necessary if I was to become wholehearted in all the Lord wanted for me, and I knew the reward would be great, but I'll be honest with you, I was extremely nervous.

The revelation experience that followed was nothing short of miraculous. I share the details in the hope that it may benefit you in your journey too.

I went into a vision over a period of three days, as Holy Spirit took me into the amazing and intricate places of my heart.

As I entered my own heart holding tightly to Holy Spirit's hand, I saw a kingdom appear before me. It was as if I had stepped back in time into a medieval period of kings and queens and elaborate castle structures. Lakes and moats provided protection around the periphery, and in the distance were high towers to shoot from, places where the approaching enemy could be seen well in advance. Tents were set like traps, ensuring that if the enemy got through, they would have to pass one test after another before they could advance further. Everything was in place so that the kingdom could withstand even the final moment of possible attack, should anyone get close enough.

I was in awe.

I enquired innocently, "Who built all of this? It looks like it's been here for ages."

"Daughter, pain has built defenses in your heart."

"Well, is this what you meant when you said that the walls of defense are coming down today?" I enquired.

The reply came: "And today we are going to bring those down. Are you ready?"

I replied, "I'm not entirely sure I am."

I felt my heart physically begin to beat rather loudly and rapidly at the news of this potential excavation. Somehow, though, I knew it was time. I could feel it within myself—every cell in my body was being shaken, and I sensed the delivery of heartache was at hand either way.

The soft gentle voice of the Lord came to me, "I am with you, remember. I have sent the Helper to be with you."

His words fell like gentle rain upon my soul, and I knew I was going to be okay.

In that moment I resigned myself to the 'process' and submitted wholeheartedly to His lead. I stood up from my seated position, tears streaming from my eyes. To the left and right of me were Jesus and Holy Spirit, holding my hands. A promise inside me began sounding, "We shall overcome!" as together we began walking towards the *Kingdom Within*.

4

HEART RESTORATION

We all have deep, dark matters of the heart, things we don't want others to know, things that we have done in our lifetime that we want kept hidden from the world, little places that we've held so deeply they become invisible, even to us sometimes. Over time, however, they begin to unravel, and eventually the truth comes out.

Now, as I entered the *Kingdom Within*, the kingdom of my own heart, I discovered its walls were built out of lies, untruths and half-truths. Stepping hand-in-hand with Holy Spirit from one area to another, I realized as I looked around the wreckage that this was not my healed heart that I was gazing upon, but my damaged heart. Venturing further towards that hidden realm, I saw the internal pain that had taken up residence within me.

In the spirit I saw a large canvas tent. It had the word 'Hurt' written across it, and a small fire was burning just outside of it. A child stepped out of the tent for a moment. She was shuddering and throwing branches on the fire, but it didn't really achieve much—it just kept the fire lit.

As I stood and watched, this 'inner child' kept retreating into the pitched tent. I wanted to reach out and help in some way, but I seemed separate and far away. Although I eagerly wanted to assist, my feet just couldn't move.

I wondered about the scene I was witnessing. If the fire was lit, why did it not provide enough heat to stop the child from shuddering? And if the child was 'free', why did she keep retreating into the tent?

It all seemed very odd.

We kept walking as I gazed in awe at the magnificence of this place and pondered how large it was. It all seemed strangely familiar. I could see that each part had been added to the next, as if the whole kingdom had been created area by area. I came across a bench seat and Holy Spirit invited me to stop and sit a while. He told me that this seat was a place for me to rest and reflect. It had been put there to provide room and comfort for my spirit to sit and watch as my heart reflected from time to time back into my childhood.

As I sat on this 'memory seat' it was like a movie reel moving at rapid speed in front of my eyes. The tent was growing foundations and changing into a tower as I aged. I felt the pain of the child within. Time and pain were working together to lay strong foundations based on the hurts of childhood, giving rise to this tower of darkness being established within.

Holy Spirit looked at my face and told me not to be sad anymore—this child was now being set free.

As soon as the tower had risen before me, the scenery changed again. Signs were placed across the front grassy area by the tower with glaring letters:

DO NOT TRESPASS

NO TRESPASSERS ALLOWED

I stared in wonder at what I was witnessing and whispered out loud, "How does this happen?"

"Oh, that's easy," came the swift answer. "The currency here is lies. You buy into the lies, and they build over the truth."

I watched in vain as huge walls arose out of the ground surrounding the tower. Holy Spirit explained that these walls were emotions built on past hurts that were not allowing new relationships to get through. I was beginning to grasp what was unfolding before me.

Next, pools of black liquid emerged, filling up the dry places, creating moats and lakes of woundedness in an attempt to prevent love from breaking in and setting the inner child free. Then I saw the hostile gatekeeper refuting every word of love and creating imaginations that were total lies. It was a fierce battle against the truth.

I stood up and moved back from the seat. I could see how everything had converged in my life. I had been set free in Christ as an adult, but the pain of my childhood still held my soul captive and my heart was still damaged. It was as if the captive child in the tent wanted to be free but had built such a strong kingdom around her that breaking down all the barriers felt like too much of a battle to overcome.

Holy Spirit revealed to me that although I had experienced healing in terms of justice and joy, now it was time for me to be totally delivered from the darkness of the *Kingdom Within*. I could see shafts of light trying to break through the atmosphere. They represented acts of kindness from others, compassion and generosity of spirit that had been shown to me over the years. Like lightning bolts, they formed holes in the atmosphere of darkness. His light was shining through, breaking into every hidden place, enabling me to carry the glory of the Kingdom of God once again.

It was time to let love in!

I could see that the child in the tent was me, and although the place I inhabited had been called 'Hurt', it was also the place of 'Innocence'. The 'branches of offense' were limited memories of the childhood trauma I had experienced. They fueled the fire itself, but never provided the warmth I needed because they held no substance to fan the flame. The offenses and hurts of such a long time ago no longer had the power within me they once had. The love of God was keeping this fire from raging, and my continued deliverance and inner healing was bringing it to an end.

Satan shoots out arrows of offense and bitterness that damage our heart, creating dark places of festering mess in the very muscle God gave us to love with.

But God is the defender of our hearts!

I came out of this vision with fresh eyes and a refreshed soul. The supernatural ability of Holy Spirit to clean up every wound and heal every infection, however long it has festered, is incredible. When we trust Him wholeheartedly, our soul can be cleansed and forever set free in the space of a moment.

This is how we begin to walk in glory realms. As we partner with God to dismantle the walls that protect our broken hearts, and allow Him to restore His true *Kingdom Within*, we experience complete transformation.

5

STRONG HEARTS

After this, Holy Spirit started speaking to me about our hearts and how they needed to become strong for the days ahead. He told me that the true *Kingdom Within* is our heart place with Him. He explained that if our hearts are not nurtured or tended to, over time they can become damaged and weakened—or, in the worst of cases, the heart can die.

In a dream, I saw how the *Kingdom Within* operates. I saw that the heart place is much like a physical heart: it has chambers that hold and pump the blood, arteries that connect the supply to the rest of body, and mechanisms to filter toxins and chemicals.

Holy Spirit showed me that we have a physical heart, an emotional heart, and a spiritual heart. The emotional heart becomes compartmentalized as we grow, storing memories and moments of pain that build up inside our hearts like cell walls. Just as arteries can become calcified and inhibit blood flow, so these cell walls in our emotional heart can divide our hearts (see

Psalm 86:11), causing the flow of life and love to become uneven, or even to shut off completely. These were the blockages He had spoken about.

As I reflected on this picture, I realized I had built cell walls in my own heart from the pain and trauma of my childhood, and now, into my adult years, the flow of love was being hindered. Holy Spirit showed me separate compartments within the chamber of the emotional heart where it was like a storage cupboard of sorts. There were drawers with labels on them that could be pulled out and examined further.

As we walked through this place, He showed me a myriad of labels such as sexual abuse, unprocessed grief, fractured relationships, rejection, family betrayal, unmet expectations, disappointment and discouragement, discontent, sibling rivalry—all manner of things that had caused damage and woundedness. Some wounds were created by words, others by acts done to me, or things I had witnessed. Some were old, some fresh and new.

I was horrified when I received a prophetic word about how suppressed memories of abuse from my childhood had caused hate in my heart. 1 John 3:15 says:

> *"Whoever hates his brother is a murderer, and you know that no murderer has eternal life abiding in him."*

Unaddressed, my emotional walls had ceased to let love in. As a result, my heart only conveyed the opposite—hatred. I was so upset and distraught that I could be a murderer, and repented in heartfelt tears, thankful to God for revealing the truth. Finally, I was able to work through the trauma and forgive all those involved.

It was akin to what happens during counseling sessions, but this was a healing moment as well. Holy Spirit showed me the processes that take place inside the *Kingdom Within*. I saw that pain leads to bitterness. Bitterness and unforgiveness in turn release physical toxins into our bodies, causing affliction and great pain.

I wanted to be wholehearted, and I believe you are reading this because God wants the same for you too.

This is your time.

I have seen firsthand the power of forgiveness to release people from the bondage of pain, both physically and emotionally. The human physical heart has limited capacity and when you put pressure on it or feed it from a wrong source it will become sick. The same is true of both the emotional and spiritual hearts. The emotional heart is often referred to as 'soul realms', and this can be, for some, a complex and layered work that takes the skill and precision of Holy Spirit to renew, heal and restore. But He can do it! Many times I have witnessed people's lives transformed overnight when the power of God is released through forgiving. It takes work and commitment at times, but it's so worth it.

My experience was like having supernatural heart surgery. At salvation, my spiritual heart had come alive. Now, through miraculous deliverance and ongoing inner healing, my emotional heart had also been resurrected.

> *"Therefore my heart is glad, and my glory rejoices"*
> Psalm 16:9

In God's heart for us there is no pain, because forgiveness reigns. So it can be for us. Our spiritual heart can be redeemed . . . and it can also be renewed! As our hearts are delivered and the healing process takes place, we become conduits of His Kingdom glory. We carry heaven to earth!

This is how we begin to walk in Glory Realms. As we experience more of God's heart, everything about us becomes a true reflection of the One we love to worship and adore.

Prayer: Holy Spirit, I come in agreement with you today, as I ask in Jesus' name, that you would come and begin to reveal and heal my heart. Pour out your revelation and show me all that is required by your grace and in your mercy to become wholehearted. In Jesus' name, Amen

PART 2

RESURRECTION POWER

6

AFFLICTED

The woman with the 'issue of blood' has no known name, but there is no doubt she was a truly desperate woman.

Let me set the scene for you.

Imagine her life. She's a young Hebrew woman, maybe twenty-five or twenty-six years old. While all her friends have been marrying, she can't even date because she's deemed 'unclean'. What an incredibly lonely life she must have had. She hardly had people lining up at her door to become friends, surely. Who wants to be friends with one who is shunned from society? In that time and culture, the fear of damaging one's reputation would have been huge—not completely unlike today, I might add.

I began to contemplate how old she may have been when her affliction started, and although we don't know exactly, I suppose she was eleven or twelve years old, around the age when young women begin to menstruate.

This transition is a turning point in every girl's life—a physical announcement as our bodies change to embrace the ability of childbearing. Later in life, another transition occurs as we experience menopause, and somewhere in between these two points is, for many, the joy of natural motherhood. For some women, however, there is neither joy nor relief at either end of their crossing over.

For the woman in Luke chapter 8, her menstrual cycle was an ongoing affliction, one that had robbed her of the joys of friendship, motherhood and the knowledge her future was secure. But she had heard of Jesus, not just as a teacher who many followed, but as a physician who healed the sick.

On the day, as Jesus was passing through her town, the young woman mustered up the courage to seek Him for her healing. The moment an opportunity for healing was offered, she drew near. This was her chance at redemption, her opportunity to be saved from her misery and to finally live well. Pushing against all social taboos, she determined to change her situation once and for all. Breaking through the crowd, she finally managed to touch the hem, or *tallit,* of His garment, the prayer tassels attached at the bottom edges of His outer robe.

I don't know about you, but I call that total courage and absolute faith!

I can imagine the indignation of the disciples towards Jesus as He stops in His tracks and, knowing power had gone out of Him, asks, "Who touched me?"

The disciples behave like it is a stupid question. Given the sheer volume of people, it could have been anyone! We hear the astonishment in their reply: "There's a crowd of people pressing in on you and all around you, hundreds even, and you ask *who?!* Who knows?!"

But Jesus responds to His disciples: "Somebody touched me, for I perceived power going out from me."

He knew it was more than just someone bumping up against Him in a crowd. This was different. This was a healing connection that took place, unlike others He had ministered. He knew someone had received healing, someone got an impartation, because He 'perceived' it. The power of heaven within Him had connected with earth in that moment. It had been drawn from Him, like water from a well.

When Jesus says, "Someone touched me," He means, "Someone purposefully came after me because they knew by faith they would be healed."

This woman, who had lived with not just monthly bleeding but a continuous blood flow from her body for many years, confesses that it was her.

Jesus replies to the woman's confession saying:

> *"Daughter, be of good cheer; your faith has made you well.*
> *Go in peace."*
> Luke 8:48

Imagine the freedom and acceptance she experiences as Christ publicly acknowledges her as "daughter." He knew she had already acknowledged in her heart that He was the Son of God, the Messiah. Now He was identifying with her, replacing her life of rejection and isolation with acceptance and intimacy. A great exchange had taken place. After twelve long years of being considered 'unclean', the woman with the issue of blood was now 'clean'. Her whole life was transformed in that one singular moment of courage and encounter with Jesus.

As I spoke with God about this woman and enquired of Him, the pages of my Bible came to life in an extraordinary way.

I realized what had taken place for her. The enemy of souls had robbed her destiny and purpose in becoming a woman, but was also intent on destroying her future by holding back her seed, her inheritance yet to come. Carrying this affliction 'for many years', had halted her potential for motherhood, hindered her chance of prosperity in the land, and stripped her of her dignity as a woman in the process.

As I sat with these thoughts, I realized that there are many women in the same situation—those who have experienced the pain and loss of their identity. How many women have been robbed of their rightful inheritance through afflictions associated with their menstrual cycle, ovaries, and their entire reproductive system? Yet God can redeem even the toughest afflictions we endure. He promises to set the captives free!

7

OVERCOMERS

In August of 2020, the Lord directed me to spend three days in seclusion with Him on a mountain top. During that time, one of the things He spoke to me was that in my next season with Him, I would "begin to walk out the word before I wrote it."

While I was studying the story of the woman with the issue of blood, the scriptures had sprung to life and her story unfolded before me until I saw it in a completely new and unexpected way. I knew Holy Spirit was beginning to show me how to receive God's power by faith, as His daughter.

I had no idea, however, that I was about to walk out my own experience of healing and faith in such a similar way . . .

The following month, I began to experience severe menstrual bleeding. By severe, I mean I would stand up and find myself covered in blood. It was hideous. I could not leave the house without taking a change of clothes and a towel to sit on in my car. It was incredibly uncomfortable and embarrassing, as well as very limiting.

At first, I cast this aside as part of menopause and thought nothing of it. I was determined to push through, as I often do. After all, life is to be lived . . . *right?* However, when it became so debilitating that I was unable to leave the house for several days at a time, I gave in to the nudging of Holy Spirit to seek medical help. By now I had experienced several months of unusually heavy and serious bleeds.

My doctor took a sample but it came back inconclusive, which was odd. Usually, the test results are clear one way or the other.

The next step was to have an ultrasound. Several years earlier, one of my ovaries had been removed. The ultrasonographer queried my paperwork, when she noticed a mass where my ovary had been. As she went further with her investigation, she revealed that there was indeed a growth of some kind, around seven centimeters in diameter, where there should have been nothing! Furthermore, there were what appeared to be small lesions on the other ovary.

Back outside the radiology building, as I was getting into my car, I felt panic rise within me as suddenly the thought entered my head, *You have cancer!*

It only crossed my mind as a possibility but immediately, the fear of the Lord came upon me and Holy Spirit spoke to me, warning me not to partner with the 'C—' word at all.

I rebuked the thought, then called a friend. Together we prayed, breaking off every thought associated with the potential of a bad report for my life, casting down every imagination, and taking every rogue thought into captivity, making them obedient to Christ (2 Corinthians 10:5). As I drove home, we simply continued praying in tongues together.

I tell you now that the enemy is a liar! He will take every opportunity to create false scenarios or beliefs in your mind to bring about his reality in your body. Thankfully, I had taken my stand against his threats, because around six o'clock that same evening, my doctor contacted me.

Doctors never ring you after hours unless it's serious, and sure enough, he sounded concerned. "Could you come in first thing in the morning for blood tests?" he asked. "I have made an urgent referral to a gynecologist who will arrange for you to be admitted to hospital as soon as possible."

My medical records now contained the words, 'suspected ovarian cancer'.

I had already agreed that I would not partner with this possible diagnosis. This was not going to be my truth! I did, however, decide to see the process through. In the meantime, I told only my family, my pastor, my mentor, and those of my 'inner circle', knowing that I could entrust such a stand of faith only to those who could stand with me and partner with God's report for my life.

Now I understood why God had led me to the story of the woman with the issue of blood. She had already tried everything else the world had to offer, but decided to place her unshakable trust in Jesus. She was ready to believe, and so was I!

The doctors were still unsure about the growth near my ovary. The gynecologist suggested a minor exploratory procedure and MRI to gather further information because the ultrasound had not provided the answers the doctors wanted. *What answer did they want?* I wondered. *What report were they seeking?* I was determined to seek and believe only a good report.

8

INHERITANCE

Having laid hold of emotional and spiritual healing, I was now determined to discover a physical healing story, one that would set me up to walk in a mighty, miraculous way.

Again, it was a story in the Bible that brought fresh revelation. This time, it was in John chapter 11. There we read of Lazarus, a friend of Jesus who had become gravely ill. His sisters had sent for Jesus, *knowing* that Jesus held the power for healing that their brother so badly needed. On hearing their request, Jesus immediately prophesied to His disciples that Lazarus's illness was not deathly, but was for the glory of God. By the time Jesus arrived at the home of Lazarus, however, his friend had been dead four days. Understandably, those nearest the family felt that if only Jesus had arrived sooner, Lazarus would have lived.

And yet, that is not the truth of this story at all.

Jesus was not late in arriving. He was *right on time*.

Lazarus's illness and death had purpose. Jesus arrived on time to bring Lazarus back from death to life. He did this so all would see and *know* the glory of God.

Interestingly, it was Martha who first expressed her firm belief in Jesus' resurrection power.

> *Now Martha said to Jesus, "Lord, if You had been here, my brother would not have died. But even now I know that whatever You ask of God, God will give You."*
> *John 11:21-22*

When Martha said, "I know" she saw beyond the physical circumstances. She saw the unseen. And sure enough, her brother was raised to life.

I had received an impartation of resurrection power which raised my heart back to life. Now, my body was about to experience that same power, *by faith!* In the physical, I had every reason to believe that I was about to embark on a long season of treatment, with no certainty of recovery. But I had determined not to partner with those thoughts. God was speaking to me through the story of Lazarus, and I was listening closely. I realized that even those with great faith still have moments of uncertainty.

In a moment of weakness, faced with the physical reality of death, Jesus reminded Martha of His promise:

> *"Did I not say to you if you would believe you would see the glory of God?"*
> *John 11:40*

Suddenly, my eyes were opened. I saw how the impossible became possible. If I would just believe, then I too would also *know* the healing, restoring, resurrection power of Christ in my physical body.

I was intrigued by the words of Jesus' prayer just before He called Lazarus to come forth from the tomb. Speaking to His Father, He said:

> *"Father, I thank You that You have heard me. And I know that You always hear Me, but because of the people who are standing by I said this, that they may believe that You sent me."*
> John 11:41-42

Martha *knew* . . . Jesus *knew* . . . and now, so did I!

I could not explain it, but somehow, *I just knew* that the growth that had been discovered in my body was not 'unto death', but that God would be glorified through it.

9

SEEING AND KNOWING

Do you remember how God had instructed me that I would walk out the word before I wrote it? Well, that's exactly what was happening.

On the next step of my journey, Holy Spirit reminded me of a woman by the name of Rahab. I had written of her in *Becoming a Daughter of the King*. Gently He instructed me to take another look at her story. There's no doubt that although we only see in part, God *knows* what we need for the journey ahead.

Rahab was the most unlikely of candidates for God's purposes. Her story is in Joshua 2-3. There we read that she was a prostitute, and yet she was chosen by God (in totally dangerous circumstances and at great peril to her own life) to help two men who had been sent by Joshua to spy out the land of Israel, especially the city of Jericho. When they arrived at Rahab's home, she stated very clearly to them:

*"I **know** that the LORD has given you the land, that the terror
of you has fallen on us, and that all the inhabitants of the land are
fainthearted because of you."*
Joshua 2:9

There it was again. *I know.*

How did she know?

The Bible tells us that Rahab had heard what God had done for the Jewish nation in bringing them out of Egypt (Joshua 2:10) and how they overcame kings and great enemies with the help of their God.

She had *heard* . . . but now she *knows*.

Something had shifted in Rahab's spirit. An exchange had taken place. Just like the woman with the issue of blood, and Martha the sister of Lazarus, Rahab had moved from *hearing* about the power of God to *knowing* it for herself.

Now it was my turn to join these women. I had heard of people being healed, and I had scriptures to lean on in faith. But something in me had shifted. I had been feeling, at times, overwhelmed and overpowered. But now, by faith, I saw beyond the circumstances. Now, I *knew* that what God had done for others, He could do for me.

Deep within my heart, I believed in the power of God, that Jesus could save, heal and restore.

Holy Spirit then impressed upon me to fast for twenty-one days. I embarked on this with a trusted and dear friend, a prayer-partner God had assigned to walk with me through this time. He gave us two scriptures to declare daily as a promise.

The first was a call to increased faith:

> Jesus replied, "Truly I tell you, if you have faith and do not doubt, not only can you do what was done to the fig tree, but also you can say to this mountain, 'Go, throw yourself into the sea,' and it will be done."
> Matthew 21:21 (NIV)

The second was a promise of increased authority:

> Behold, I give you the authority to trample on serpents and scorpions, and over all the power of the enemy, and nothing shall by any means hurt you.
> Luke 10:19

Sometime around the end of the fast, I had a dream. In the dream, the Lord told me to lay my hands on the area of my body that was under attack and simply declare with faith and authority, "You are removed in Jesus' name."

When I woke up, I did exactly that, as I wasn't sure if the declaration had been made in the dream, or if the dream was an instruction. It didn't matter. The moment I laid my hand on the place where the growth had been found and declared it gone, I *knew* by faith that the growth had been removed and I would not be having surgery.

At the prompting of Holy Spirit, I chased down the test results I had been waiting for and received the good report that there were no cancerous markers in my blood. *Hallelujah!*

The specialist still felt that surgery was necessary. The excessive bleeding continued, and she wanted to investigate further, remove the growth, and address the endometrial thickness in my uterus.

What happened next is confirmation that when we *know* what God has done and refuse to partner with lying symptoms that seek to steal our faith, healing power can flow.

As soon as I received a letter in the mail for the planned surgery, I said, "No! That's not happening. It's gone!"

Holy Spirit then prompted me to call about the date for my MRI booking. As a result, I was able to jump the public queue and was allocated an MRI in a private facility that had been contracted to fulfill public wait-lists. With no effort at all, I convinced them to move the MRI date, so it came before the scheduled surgery.

I went in for the MRI and soon after, received the results:

> *Endometrial thickness is normal. No polyp or mass lesion visible. No significant abnormality identified.*

I was ecstatic! When I rang the hospital to cancel the surgery, I was told that I had beaten the specialist, and that she had to review the results before making that decision—to which I laughed and said over the phone, "God has made it for her!"

A nurse called me later that day. "The gynecologist has reviewed your results. There was no growth visible on the MRI, so there will be no need for surgery," she said. "The specialist will prepare a discharge letter."

"What do you mean, there is no growth? How did it just disappear?" I asked the nurse. Of course, she could offer no explanation, so I asked her to have the specialist call me herself to confirm and explain the results.

The next day the gynecologist called me, but when I asked her how the thickness and growth had disappeared, she had no explanation to offer. She simply said that sometimes this sort of thing happens, and good on me for being such a strong advocate for my own health.

I asked her to put that in writing! And so, she did. In November 2020 the pronouncement was spoken and written over my life: *Suspected ovarian cancer.* By February 2021, just three months later, the growth had miraculously and mysteriously disappeared, and I received a discharge letter confirming the cancellation of my planned hysteroscopy. The letter stated: *". . . no evidence of polyps or other masses."*

This is the power of *knowing*. To this day, I remain healed of my 'issue of blood'. I did not and do not have any cancer at all. But most of all, my faith has moved to an unshakable place in God.

10

MINISTERING IN FAITH

The first time I encountered Jesus, it was in a movie theatre. I didn't have the same need or expectations as the woman with the issue of blood. I didn't know how badly I needed Him, and I didn't run to Him with a heart full of faith. But like the woman in Luke 8, it was the same one touch from Jesus that transformed my life. As I watched *The Passion of the Christ*, it was as if He came to me, and in an instant I knew that He was the Son of God and that He possessed power to heal.

The impartation I received in that moment was what Jesus had recognized as the 'power of God going out of Him'. I received an extraordinary 'gift' of faith. This meant that even in my earliest days of walking with Christ, miracles and healing seemed very normal to me. By faith, I could 'see' the breakthrough others longed for. When God showed me something in the spirit, it was real to me; even if it had not yet happened, I fully believed it was possible.

Receiving physical healing in my own body required a combination of 'seeing' and 'knowing'. This led to a new level of faith. As I continued to go deeper with God, I perceived He had even bigger plans for me. The fruit of my twenty-one-day fast was becoming evident. My authority in the spirit had indeed grown.

As I walked this out with the Lord, I discovered something interesting. Everywhere I went I began hearing of people with ovarian cancer. I had seen this pattern in the lives of other ministers and friends of faith—whatever they had personally experienced became the area where they were able to minister with new levels of authority and effectiveness.

When a close ministry colleague began her own journey with chemotherapy, I found myself able to stand in great authority and believe God's report in a new and more determined way than my faith had allowed for in the past. Deep within I just knew that He would get all the glory and that an amazing testimony was being birthed through her.

I also noticed that as I began to share my own testimony with those the Lord directed me to, I was invited to speak and minister in new environments. My faith rose in anticipation, but the first thing I understood was that God's timing is everything.

On one occasion, my speaking engagement was postponed twice, but on the third date, what took place was just like the story of Lazarus. The people who came that time were desperate for healing, and like Martha, 'just knew' that the power of God was present to call forth life. I had incredible faith and strength in the Lord on that occasion, and Holy Spirit brought healing and release to those who were present. There was also a great hunger for others to know His healing power—in fact, people grabbed whatever items they could, and together we prayed over them, believing for miraculous healings to take place even after we left the room.

I realized later that these people weren't simply running to Jesus for healing in their bodies; they were also coming for an impartation of boldness, courage and faith to believe for their friends and relatives who were suffering. They were being drawn to a source of faith, just as the woman in Luke 8 was drawn to Jesus because of the power He carried. This is resurrection power at work!

What a joy it is to minister the healing power of heaven. Soon, I was meeting women who were experiencing all sorts of gynecological issues.

One young woman, whom I had mentored in her teen years, came to see me. She was now grown up, newly married, and planning for an increase in her household as she and her young husband happily embarked on life as a couple.

When we met, Holy Spirit revealed something to me of her hopes and desires to become a mother. As we talked further, I discovered that fear lay inside her. From the time she had begun getting her period, she had experienced very painful episodes of endometriosis, and had been told that getting pregnant would be difficult, if it happened at all.

Well, you can easily guess my position on that statement. *Oh no, you don't, Devil!*

We sat and prayed, and I shared the testimony of God's goodness in my own life. Giving thanks to God, we came into agreement for a pregnancy to take place in God's perfect will and timing. As we prayed, I received a prophetic word that by the following September, she would be pregnant. Imagine our joy when I heard the news that my young friend was pregnant—and that indeed it happened in September.

Glory to God!

11

GOD'S DAUGHTERS

As my heart came back to life, I had the joy of meeting others who had experienced the resurrection power of Jesus.

I met one such woman in Cambodia. Her name was Thun.

She writes:

> *In September 2019, I found a little lump on my right breast. I went to at least seven hospitals to consult with specialists before they discovered that I had a tumor which had to be removed urgently.*
>
> *I felt scared and shocked about this result. Suddenly, the world became dark. I had been married just over three years, and I had two boys just 1 1/2 and 2 1/2 years old. My chest was tense, I had difficulty breathing, and death seemed to be closing in. I hid my tears from my family, but I was worried. I tried to hang onto my faith and keep looking to God. I started to pray and asked Jesus to give me life so I could continue to live with my*

husband and children.

I was fearful when I went in for surgery four months later, but the team of doctors prayed for me before the operation, and I felt some relief.

When the results of the biopsy came in, and I was told I had stage 3 cancer, the fear returned. My tears started to fall, and I couldn't speak. My hands were shaking, and I felt discomfort in my heart. All my physical and emotional strength was gone. I was facing twelve rounds of chemotherapy, and I was scared. In that moment, I lost interest. Fear was the only feeling I had.

A few days later, after receiving a more detailed explanation from the doctor, my husband and I decided I should proceed with the chemotherapy treatment.

When the chemo entered my body, it felt as if a hundred hot needles were piercing my face. My head hurt as if someone was pulling my hair from behind. I lost my sense of taste; even water seemed bitter. I began to feel afraid of eating and drinking. After each round of chemotherapy I vomited for two days, almost every half an hour. Sometimes, diarrhea, vomiting, and stomachaches happened all at the same time. It was a most difficult time for me.

In the hot season in Phnom Penh between March to May, I started to experience difficulty in breathing, as well as the vomiting. I moved to a cooler place in the hope I would feel better, but it didn't help. I was terrified I might die of a heart attack, so I wore lose fitting clothes and no bra just so that I could breathe. The doctor advised me to take medication for my stomach, and sleeping pills to help me sleep at night, but I just couldn't. On top of the chemotherapy, it was too much for me.

After the sixth round of chemotherapy, the side effects were so intense that I was unable to return home after each treatment. I felt sorry for my children every time I prepared my bag to stay at the hospital. My little sons cried, "Mummy, please don't go to hospital. I want to be with you! Mummy, please don't be sick. I'll help you." This broke my heart and made me cry, but the side effects were unmanageable. I vomited until my body and heart rate became weak, my skin became darker, and my hair fell out at such a rate that I was afraid to even wash it.

When my hair fell out, I became very depressed. Unable to accept what was happening, I couldn't even look at myself in the mirror. In terrible pain, I just wailed in the bathroom. I remembered the doctor telling me that these side effects were normal for patients undergoing chemotherapy but that didn't make it any easier for me to accept. I felt so ashamed of my hair loss. It was hard having people stare at me, knowing I was a cancer patient. I didn't want to be pitied by others; this only made me feel weaker.

By the time I got to the tenth and eleventh round of treatment, I was like a robot. I couldn't move my neck or head. I needed my husband to put me to bed at night and lift me up in the morning. It felt like my weak body didn't belong to me anymore. I started to feel useless and a burden to my family.

I was young, but I felt like an old person. I didn't have enough white blood cells to function properly. I tried eating nutritional food, but that did not restore the levels of white blood cells I needed. I was blessed that my husband had good health coverage for our family, because medical care is unaffordable for most people in Cambodia. Even so, my only option was to receive an injection, which cost the same as a full round of chemotherapy. The problem was, if I continued with chemotherapy without adequate white blood cells, my spine could be badly affected.

Right before I was about to start the twelfth round of chemotherapy, I caught the flu. Seeing I had developed a fever, the doctor advised me not to delay chemotherapy even though my white blood cell count was low. I couldn't imagine how I could handle this final treatment. All my joints were painful, and yet I didn't want to delay, so I prayed for a miracle.

We were in the middle of the Covid-19 pandemic, which meant that the hospital organized and checked the body temperature of anyone who wanted to enter the hospital. With a temperature of 40°C. I thought the security guards wouldn't let me in. I had red spots all over my body, and my face was red with fever. I used a wet towel to help reduce my body temperature, but that meant my shirt was wet when I arrived at the hospital. The miracle was that I was so weak and tired that when I went through the front doors, it was as if the security guards didn't see me. I sat in the chair and was almost asleep while I waited to see the doctor.

I was surprised when the results came back that my white blood cells were high enough for the final chemotherapy. I knew God had allowed this to happen. His power was at work, giving strength to my body when I had none of my own.

I was relieved when the chemotherapy finally came to an end. By God's grace I had finished the first stage. Now I had to await a CT-scan.

As the date for the CT-scan approached, fear overtook me once again. I cried thinking that if the result wasn't good, I would have to receive more chemotherapy.

What a surprise when I found that the cancer had not spread. I was very excited! My organs were clear, and there was no need for further chemotherapy. The doctor recommended I take a prescribed dose every day *for five years and have regular checks every six months, but I was able to return home. The tumors had been reversed! Glory to God!*

Thun's story is evidence that as daughters of God, we are loved beyond measure. With one touch Jesus can raise us from death to life, both in heart and body. When Thun first started losing her hair, she felt ashamed as a woman, socially outcast and unacceptable. Just like many of the other women who came to Jesus for healing, she felt like hiding away. It is remarkable to me that despite the fear Thun experienced through her journey with cancer, she remained steadfast in faith that God was with her through it all.

Since then, Thun has become a spiritual 'daughter' to me. She has learned to draw on the strength of the Lord in difficult times, and to believe God's promises about healing. Jeremiah 30:17 says, "But I will restore you to health and heal your wounds" (NIV).

In times of suffering, Thun pronounced these truths. Today she knows the power of agreement in prayer. In fact, after we prayed together, along with another friend, Thun's hair loss was reversed, and today she is growing hair again!

Thun also experienced God's provision, both through her husband and insurance company, and through the generosity of God's people. As a result of walking through tremendous suffering, Thun's faith has been strengthened. "God had a plan," she says. "He took suffering from my heart and allowed me to draw closer to Him."

Just like the woman with the issue of blood, Jesus spoke into Thun's heart and called her 'daughter'. Today, Thun wants every woman to know that His great love and mercy can triumph in the face of fear, and that we can overcome all things in and through Christ Jesus.

Following her ordeal, Thun discovered a new part of herself she never knew existed. She began baking and creating desserts as a way of expressing her thanks to those who helped and served her and her family during their time of need.

It has been a pleasure in recent times to partner with Thun in prayer and finances as she established a bakery as a means of sharing the love of God with the people of Cambodia. This was a long-forgotten dream from her childhood, one which God resurrected in her as she healed. Today, Thun is thriving, and so is her family. She brings joy to all those she serves with her amazing creations.

Thun's story is not unlike the story that could be told by many women who have suffered the effects of cancer and the horrifically painful treatment so often associated with it. But the recovery she experienced is also shared by countless women. God's resurrection power is at work in His daughters!

PART THREE

RESURRECTION LIFE

12

A LITTLE OIL

The Lord is my strength and my shield; My heart trusted in Him, and I am helped; Therefore my heart greatly rejoices, And with my song I will praise Him.
Psalm 28:7

Having received emotional and spiritual renewal, a physical healing in my body, and an impartation of faith to see miracles in the lives of others, I felt I had more than enough. I had come full circle. God had gathered all my fragments and broken pieces and re-created my heart.

He also entrusted me with the stewardship of my own heart.

If I were to fulfill God's call on my life, two things were required of me: To continually increase my capacity for faith, and to keep my heart clean.

One day, my friend and mentor, Jennifer Eivaz, asked, "Do you have the heart for what God has called you to?"

She explained that a small heart leads to a small life, a broken heart leads to a broken life, and a dead heart cannot minister life to others."

Then she said to me, "Nobody else can carry what you carry. But God needs your heart to be clean if you are to carry it all."

Her words resonated with me. I understood it was my job to keep my renewed heart clean. I was responsible for ensuring it remained a conduit for His blessings and promises.

The next time I heard God calling me to "come up to the mountain" to spend time alone with Him, I knew I was to stay there until I had received everything the Lord wanted to show me. Finding the perfect location, I locked myself inside a cabin in the mountains and decided I would not even open the door until I had received all He intended for me.

For three days, I went on an extraordinary journey in the spirit. I turned the lock on the door, unpacked my bags, and laid out my writing implements ready to receive whatever Holy Spirit would speak. At that point, I noticed a small wooden flask with oil inside, and a sparrow etched into the wood. I picked it up and delighted in its simple yet beautiful existence.

The sparrow holds special meaning for me. I looked at the beautiful etching, and knew that just as God takes care of a sparrow's every need, so He had taken care of me . . . and He would continue to do so. I could trust Him.

As I laid the tiny flask next to my writing pad and picked up my pen, Holy Spirit began to breathe life on my writing, and I found myself caught up in the story of the prophet Elisha.

Closing my eyes momentarily, I saw a vision of a small hut and a man resting.

I reached for my Bible and felt led to the book of 2 Kings, chapter 4. As I opened the pages, the scene before me suddenly sprung to life.

I could see the widow whose husband had passed away, leaving her alone with two sons and a huge debt. Like any mother in a similar situation, she probably looked around her to see what she could do to prevent a bad outcome. But there was nothing; no one who could help her financially. All she had was this one jar of oil. This woman had been thrust into a desperate situation. Her husband had died owing money, a debt that now fell on her and her sons. The creditor had already arranged to take her two sons as payment. If the debt remained outstanding, they would become his slaves. Then he could do with them whatever he pleased, treat them however he wanted.

But Elisha the prophet gives her instructions which could remove her debt and the potential bondage she was facing. She has only one thing left: a flask of oil. The Hebrew phrase is, "but a flask of oil." In all likelihood, this means it was a very small amount.

"Go!" Elisha says to her. "Get vessels from everywhere. Get empty vessels. Borrow them if you have to. Just get as many as you can."

He's sending her out to do something. If she wants to receive her miracle, she has to take action.

In an act of faith, she chooses to be simply obedient to the task at hand. The prophet has not yet explained what she is to do with these empty vessels. She is operating in 'blind faith' at this point, unable to see the outcome. She is simply trusting his instruction. Like the woman with the issue of blood, she is desperate. Desperation creates a sense of abandon. She'll do whatever he says. But also like the woman in Luke 8, she somehow *knows* it is the right thing to do. She's not questioning the command. It's as if her spirit understands that the prophet is setting her up for blessing. She's getting the message that *this is going to be big!*

When God gives a command like this, don't focus for a moment on what you don't have. Just make room for what you *will* have!

It is interesting to me that next, the prophet tells the widow and her two sons that they must do something together, as a family. "Shut the door," he says. Together they gather, just the three of them. The outside world doesn't get to see what is about to happen as they press into the word of the prophet to "pour out the oil."

In faith, the widow of 2 Kings 4 takes all that she has, a little jar of oil, and begins to pour it into the jars she has collected. Can you picture her standing there pouring out from her tiny flask into container after container? I imagine her sons just trying to keep up, moving one full vessel after another to the side until the flow ceases.

I don't know about you and your family, but I can tell you, my children and I would be screaming in amazement and rejoicing in wonder at this point, that's for sure!

The thing is, no one else did it for her; she had to do it for herself. But as she did, a miracle took place. God met her in that moment and brought multiplication to her situation, but the miracle was poured out from her hands. One after the other, all the vessels got filled, and only then did the flow of oil cease.

But there's more to this miracle story. Interestingly, 2 Kings 4:6 in the Hebrew scriptures reads, "the oil stood up." This is not a physical 'standing up'. It refers to the commodity markets rising. Not only does the widow have something to trade; it has miraculously increased in value. This is no mere pay-your-debts story. It's an abundantly-ever-after story!

Opening the door, the woman goes back out to Elisha and tells him all that has taken place. "Go!" he says. "Sell the oil and pay your debts. You and your sons can live on what is left" (2 Kings 4:7, NIV).

What a dignified way to be released from her shame and bondage. She takes the oil as a commodity, and trades it for her freedom—and the freedom of future generations! With that, she is released. By the time she returns home the debt that was hanging over them all has been paid, her sons are delivered from a life of slavery, and the family has more than enough. Their story has changed. No longer are they destitute or enslaved; instead, they are set free to live a life of abundance.

What a lesson for you and me. God has placed his oil of joy within us. I already have it, and so do you. I know all too well that it can sometimes feel as if the oil has run dry. In our most desperate moments, the hardest thing to do is to walk in faith and obedience. It's the most natural thing to look to others for help. But I want you to know this: you don't need anyone else to perform the miracle for you. You have the power of heaven within you to see your own miracle come to pass. God provided for this woman, and He has already made provision for you as well.

As I reflected on the story of the widow with the flask of oil, God brought to the surface a deep fear within my heart. My own past and hidden shame had left a debt, one I did not want my children to pay for, and yet I had projected my fears onto them. Now I wanted to shut them inside my heart with me, to await the miracle of deliverance from the debt.

God was expanding my heart for the miraculous. He was asking me to increase my capacity beyond what I currently had—to make space for increased levels of faith. He wanted to repair the damages of the past and pour out enough restoration oil that I could settle my debts, not only for myself and my family, but for others too.

I believe it is time for heart restoration in all our lives. It is time for our damaged past to become just that: past. It only takes one miracle for our past losses to be recompensed. One miracle can restore our hopes and dreams. Provision has already been made!

Prayer: Heavenly Father, I thank you for the wisdom of your prophetic word that set the widow free from her debt and created miraculous provision for her family and community and I ask, Holy Spirit, that you would come now and move miraculously on me, my family, and my community to do the same again for us all as you did for her. We receive this gift from you by faith and thank you for Your miraculous provision in all things. In Jesus' name, Amen.

13

FULL INHERITANCE

When I went up the mountain with God, I wasn't expecting to be immersed in the story of the widow with the flask of oil. Now I began to realize that there was more at stake than my own healing, freedom and anointing. God was intent on delivering my full inheritance.

Reflecting on the account in 2 Kings 4, I saw that it is in desperate times that the enemy of our hearts is most likely to steal, kill and destroy. Certainly, he was trying to destroy this family. If he could ruin their prospects, rob them of the legacy of their husband and father who had served the prophet, tarnish their reputation, and deprive future generations of their inheritance, there was a chance he could steal their faith as well.

Without faith and hope, our hearts can die.

God is a restorer of fortunes, the One who lays up an inheritance for His people.

In my life, an inheritance had gone astray.

The loss of my earthly father had left me with many layers of grief to work through. Part of that grief was that a monetary debt had been left, one that was not mine to pay. As I worked through the story of the widow's oil, I saw that I had a part to play, however, in ensuring the debt did not fall upon me or my family in other ways.

From the mountain top I made a phone call. It was a difficult conversation, but God's grace and mercy were at work through me. As a result, my father's debt that had fallen upon his widow was paid, and the good faith between bloodlines restored. Praise God!

It does not matter what is owed to us, when we do what is right and pay our debts in full, His righteousness in us is restored, and so is His justice.

After that phone call, I felt such release. From that point on, future generations in my family could move forward in the inheritance of God's grace. The walls of the *Kingdom Within* were being restored! That night as I rested, God spoke to me in dreams and visions and when I woke, my soul and spirit were refreshed with new revelation and encouragement.

The following day, God disclosed another aspect of my internal kingdom.

I had taken a break from writing to admire the view from the mountain top and share with my dear friend and prayer partner about the tiny flask I had discovered with the sparrow on it and the subsequent revelation I had received.

As we spoke, God showed me that what I had just walked through and seen was about a call on my life to set captives free from both physical and spiritual debt. I heard Holy Spirit say, "Sharon, I have called you to be a light in dark places and to those held in darkness."

The words of Isaiah 61:3 and Luke 4:18 are written in my heart. I have been created to set the captives free and I *'know'* it. This is my calling, and now that my own heart had been resurrected, I could accept it wholeheartedly. I know who I am, but I also know that I am just one of many who are lights forged in the fire to bring deliverance to those bound in darkness.

The Word of the Lord

When we receive the word of the Lord into our lives, everything changes.

My final revelation on the mountain came through the Word of God, this time through the story of another widow—the widow of Sidon.

In 1 Kings 17:8, the 'word of the Lord' came to the prophet Elijah. The Hebrew text makes it clear that God was speaking directly to Elijah.

"Get up and go," He told the prophet. Then He assures Elijah that He has made provision for the journey and prepared the way ahead of him.

Now it was Elijah's responsibility to arise and take action.

Interestingly, in this instance, God chose a widow to take care of the prophet—not the other way around.

This widow, however, does not worship the same God as Elijah, nor is she of his culture. She is from Sidon. *Scandalous!*

But God is clear. Elijah is to get up and go to Sidon, a land that is dealing with drought and famine. Elijah had been sitting in the place of provision and now God is sending him to the land of lack! *Ouch!*

Suddenly, the words in my Bible sprang to life.

Elijah arrives at the gates of a city. Seeing a woman, he asks her to bring him water and bread. She explains to this stranger that she only has enough for one last meal for herself and her son; after they have eaten that, they are planning only to lay down and die. There is no more food. This is to be their last meal.

Elijah responds by telling the widow to continue with her preparation, gathering sticks for a fire, but to be sure to set aside a small loaf for him in the process. Can you imagine the fear and vulnerability this woman must have felt in that moment? She is alone with this foreign man who is telling her she must feed him when she is preparing for death. I imagine she is weak from lack of food; she's gathering sticks alone, which means she has no help. She doesn't have enough to cook twice, only once. And so she replies to the prophet, "I only have a little oil and a little flour."

Like the widow of 2 Kings 4, there is *only a little* to work with.

But unlike the previous story, the prophet gives her a promise to cling to. In 1 Kings 17:14 we read:

> *"For thus says the Lord God of Israel: 'The bin of flour shall not be used up, nor shall the jar of oil run dry, until the day the Lord sends rain on the earth.'"*

God's provision never runs dry!

This provision promised to the widow continued until the drought that had caused the famine was broken. This drought was approximately three years long! For that entire period of time, the woman, her son, Elijah, and her whole community, ate supernaturally in a time of famine. They did not die, they lived. Again, the outcome was abundance.

Because of the prophet's obedience, not only was he taken care of, but he was able to bless a woman who had great need. Once again, God wanted to rescue a woman who was desperate, and once again, the next generation was saved.

God is in the business of restoring our futures and redeeming our inheritance.

At the Word of the Lord, the prophet received anointing for increase, and through his obedience, he honored that anointing and the gift was multiplied. The widow, too, had to respond in faith. At the request of the prophet, she sacrificed a portion of her last meal, and in doing so received incredible multiplication. This is the path from death to life. This is resurrection power!

Obedience Brings Blessing

As I dialogued with Holy Spirit, I heard Him say, "Ask. Just ask, and you shall receive."

"What can I do Lord?" I responded.

"Do what Elijah did," He told me. "Be my voice. Bring the word from the Lord that provokes a turnaround. Deliver people from death to life and abundant blessing."

"To whom shall I go, Lord?"

"Go to women, the widows of this world, and the fatherless. Go and set the captives free."

Widening my spiritual lens, I was awakened to the possibilities rather than hindered by the limitations of predetermined vision.

It is one thing to be called, but then you must start to walk out that calling and understand what it might look like. I was determined to stay firmly within my lane as I navigated the path ahead. It helped to see a correlation between my own calling and the stories God had highlighted to me. I noticed that the story God had written over my lifetime always involved women and children, and their plight of desperation. I also had a heart for entire communities to be blessed, just as the widow women in scripture had been a catalyst for the blessing of their communities.

With renewed clarity I saw that women globally are as much at the center of their communities as men. Often these women have been positioned to welcome cultural transformation. Through their own personal hardship, they have encountered God's voice and receive a blessing of multiplication that enables those around them to flourish with abundant miraculous provision.

Deep in my spirit, these stories resonated with what I sensed the Lord was calling me to. As a mother I could identify with the hopelessness of the widow in the story with Elijah. The emotions this woman must have been feeling as she went about gathering the sticks that would light the final fire in her son's life and bring death to him as she prepared the last meal they were ever to have together would have been overwhelming.

I thought of all the mothers of sick and dying children who have asked themselves what they could have done better, what they could have repented from, that would have made the situation regarding their children different.

But looking for someone to blame does nothing to help. God alone is our provider. He is Jehovah Jireh, the One who sustains all life, and He can bring a turn-around to any situation. Even when we don't know Him, God can and will send someone for us. I think that years of food being provided from 'a little oil and flour' would have been enough for me, but God gives abundance.

I am forever grateful for the people God has sent into my life over many years and for those He continues to send. Now I have been sent as a prophetic voice to write in the hope that through my stories and revelations you will receive your freedom and provision too. I have been given a blessing in order to be a blessing; that is how I see the prophetic call of God working out in my life today. By faith I declare unlimited favor over your life today!

But the breakthrough would never have come if Elijah was not first willing to leave the place of rest and supernatural provision, sacrificing his comfort to minister to others. I feel called to a similar posture. But that was only the beginning.

One evening, I had a visitation from what I am quite certain was an angelic being. It was not a figure as such; what I experienced was a hue, a glow of iridescent light that moved and yet stayed still all at once. Though it is difficult to articulate, I want to try and describe this for you, because many speak of angelic visitations in the shape and form likened to human beings. This manifestation, however, was something quite different. A glowing being was inside my room. I did not hear an audible voice, but I did hear in my spirit these words:

> *"This is your commissioning from God, to go out from this place in power, to speak as the Lord's voice from heaven on earth, to heal the broken-hearted and*

set the captives free."

That night I slept incredibly well and dreamed beautiful dreams of people's lives being transformed and whole communities saved.

About nine months after that encounter, I was in a random country church when a man approached me after a service with what he said was a sense of urgency to deliver a word from the Lord to me. He simply said, "Your prophetic voice is needed." I had told no-one about the visitation or what had been spoken to me, so this was a very encouraging confirmation. The prophet's word was recognized as God's word, not his own. When he spoke, it was with God's authority and God's voice.

God was assuring me that I too could be confident in the call of God to be His voice and to carry His authority as I released His words into the lives of others. I was beginning to understand the fullness of the call, to recognize that God had been training me through visions, dreams, and His word. Like the prophet, not everything made sense to me at first, and it may not to you either, but as we walk in obedience to God's call and take up the mantle on our lives, we can trust He has a greater purpose in mind, a purpose to multiply blessing to others.

14

PROMISED LAND

"Now when He was asked by the Pharisees when the kingdom of God would come, He answered them and said, "The kingdom of God does not come with observation; nor will they say, 'See here!' or 'See there!' For indeed, the kingdom of God is within you."
Luke 17:20-21

We carry the Kingdom of Heaven within us, and as we fully surrender totally abandoned and complete within our hearts, we will see the power of God move in miraculous ways across the earth. My hope for you is that you will take your place as an overcomer. May the faith we carry match the authority that lies within each of us as sons or daughters in the Glory Kingdom. Our faith has got to rise to the level of the word that we put faith in—God's Word. Let's combine faith and authority in order to bring God's heart to all people everywhere.

My greatest discovery about leading with an equal measure of faith and authority came from the book of Joshua. Like the Israelites, God had already given me an inheritance and a family, but now I really needed to *see* it. I needed to 'cross over' into the place and promises God had for me. And like Joshua, I came up against some walls. These were not walls of my own making—the *Kingdom Within* had already been conquered. This time, the walls were in front of me.

The year I turned fifty, I was experiencing God's favor in all the areas of my life. Having worked as an independent artist for many years, I received a contract to deliver art services in the prisons of my region of New Zealand. Equally unexpected was an offer from an anti-trafficking organization to spend two years delivering art therapy services and training to counselors in Cambodia. I had previously explored this opportunity and been denied; now they came looking for me! It was a real sign of restoration.

And then, I received an invitation to travel to Nairobi for a three-week arts mission, all expenses paid. Suddenly, Holy Spirit reminded me that as a child, I had dreamed of going to Africa. God was fulfilling the dreams of my heart, even those I had forgotten and given up on. His resurrection power on this childhood dream He had planted within me gave me such a love for Africa as a nation and its people.

In the months of preparation for the trip to Nairobi, God began to speak to me more regularly and directly than ever before.

I have always said to people, "Prayer is just a conversation, so why don't you have one?" Now I was having conversations with God continually, and the words began to flow very freely. I wrote in my journal: "I cannot deny you. It is Christ that lives, not I."

Holy Spirit responded:

"It is Christ in you that lives, yes. We are on holy ground. Everywhere we go, we go as three, 'Three-in-thee'. You are holy ground. You are in me, and I am in you. Everywhere we go, we go together. Everything you see, you see as me. You are with me, and I am with you. We are together. I never leave. I live in you. You live in me. You have died, and I remain. It is me who lives! It is me who lives in and through you. Get hold of this, Sharon, this oneness, this indwelling, it's important."

Everything He was speaking was in my Bible.

"I no longer live, but Christ lives in me. The life I now live in the body, I live by faith in the Son of God, who loved me and gave himself for me"
Galatians 2:20 (NIV)

I grabbed hold of what He was saying.

And then, God spoke to me through a prophetic word, saying that I would lead others into their 'promised land'. My mind went to the book of Joshua, and as I leaned into the story of that one man's leadership, it was as if the inheritance of Holy Spirit became amplified in my life in a way I had not known previously.

I sensed that God wanted to move me from a place of looking for supernatural provision to a place of ongoing provision, just as He did for the people of Israel.

"Then the manna ceased on the day after they had eaten the produce of the land; and the children of Israel no longer had manna, but they ate the food of the land of Canaan that year."
Joshua 5:12

The manna ceased because the Israelites had crossed over into a place of sustained provision. The 'new land' they were about to enter had more produce available to them than ever before. They had manna from heaven to sustain them on the journey, but as Holy Spirit was showing me, up ahead was an area of *'greater than'* provision.

Like the widows of 2 Kings, God's people had to move from a place of reliance to a place of abundance. There was variety and more on offer in the natural than they had ever heard of or experienced so far. And so it is for us. We must not get hung up on the supernatural and thus limit ourselves to the place of reliance. We need to move beyond our experience and into the place of expectation. Believe for something new, refreshing, different, interesting, and *greater than* what you already know. Dare to dream and imagine what your full inheritance looks like!

This is heaven's strategy for us. Joshua gained heaven's perspective as he sought God on how to battle, and it changed the way he approached the future. This time, he would not need to fight in the ways of old, or rely on what had been done in the past. Instead, he positioned an army before and behind the priests as they blew the trumpets according to God's instructions. In the same manner, as I prepared to go out in obedience to the Lord's leading towards Africa, I was assured there was an army at both my front and rear guard.

In the meantime, I was in prayer for my upcoming trip when God spoke to me about the need to 'stand up in new garments'. I had received this from the Lord some years earlier, but as I began my journey of crossing over from reliance on God to receiving my full inheritance, the Lord revealed to me something incredible. He showed me that the new garments He had promised to 'stand me up in' had been woven from my heartfelt praise and worship during the time I had spent out of ministry, and that it was this intimacy with Him that had cultivated His glory in me. Now I could see the garments prepared for me—beautiful cloaks of beaming light that had been sewn together in the spiritual realms, awaiting my embrace.

Around that time, I attended a meeting where the speaker laid hands on me, imparting an anointing for the raising of the dead. She had received this anointing in Switzerland from the granddaughter of Smith Wigglesworth, the renowned evangelist and healing minister.

Sometimes we receive a word of knowledge or encouragement in a meeting. At other times I find God speaks in miraculous and unusual ways through a movie or a book, but more often, His word comes directly to us as we spend time in the presence of God, listening. In any case, as I put these moments together in my mind, I sensed God was encouraging me and preparing me for what He knew lay ahead of me. God wanted me to 'see' what He wanted to do, and then I could follow with total confidence as I headed to Kenya.

And the Lord said to Joshua: "See! I have given Jericho into your hand, its king, and the mighty men of valor."
Joshua 6:2

God wanted Joshua to focus his eyes, and see Jericho already delivered, already conquered, already given to him. Then the Lord showed him the steps that would bring it to pass:

> "It shall come to pass, when they make a long blast with the ram's horn, and when you hear the sound of the trumpet, that all the people shall shout with a great shout; then the wall of the city will fall down flat. And the people shall go up every man straight before him."
> Joshua 6:5

I was excited about what lay ahead. Like Joshua, I wanted to lay hold of what God was going to do—to step into what was yet to be done as if it had already happened.

And then right before I left for the mission trip, a friend gave me a word of warning: "Don't forget," she said, "that after they crossed into the Promised Land was when the fighting began. They had to take what had been promised. They had to fight for it."

My friend told me that in a dream she saw herself standing with her sword raised, defending me, and promised to pray daily for me while I was away. That dream had more merit than either of us realized at the time. When another intercessor contacted me, saying she had seen my face become the lion of Judah, I was intrigued. "People will see Him in you," she said, "and any witchcraft that comes near you will flee."

About now I was beginning to sense that along with all the hopes and expectations I had for this trip, something else was waiting for me that wasn't totally good. In the end, I decided it best to abandon all expectations and just be prepared for whatever came my way.

15

GARMENTS OF MAJESTY

As my feet stepped onto African soil for the first time, I began to understand and claim the fullness of my inheritance. He had once again made a way where there had seemed no way. He was restoring my heart as a missionary and an adventurer for Jesus, full of faith and promises. I felt alive again! Resurrected! I was walking in my true identity.

I liken identity to clothing. In times of sadness and grief we often put on garments of heaviness. They change our posture and keep us wrapped up in whatever sorrow we have encountered. But in Isaiah 61:3, God promises to exchange those garments for the garments of praise.

In *Becoming a Daughter of the King*, I wrote of a time in my life where everything was stripped away. At that time, I felt as if I was in a pit of despair. My identity had to be rebuilt in the secret place with God. I needed to see the truth of what God had been doing, and take on the identity of a 'risen one' — one who had known the reality of His resurrection power.

It's easy to think of resurrection power as an impartation to run out and start raising corpses to life, but the things of God are not the ways of man. The resurrection power of God in me needed to manifest in my own life before I could bring it to others. Bringing dead hearts to life is no simple task and it takes the surgical expertise of Holy Spirit. We need to let Him train us with wisdom for the process.

As I entered Nairobi, I was aware that it was time to put on the garments of His majesty that had been awaiting me and claim my full inheritance. Ahead of me lay a new season of leadership, one in which I needed to partner with God's ways rather than what I had done in the past. I had a deep assurance that my time in Africa would cultivate in me gifts of good leadership and reveal the qualities that God was wanting to cultivate in me, just like Joshua.

I had only been on the ground four days when the unknown attack I had suspected was waiting for me, began to surface. I was so glad that God had built me up and fortified me with His Word. There is nothing quite like being in another nation without all your familiar supports around you when spiritual warfare breaks out!

In this case, the attack was spiritual, but it came through one of my counterparts.

Unbeknown to me, I had been invited to Africa with an agenda, not my agenda, nor God's. The purpose was to see if I might be the one who would take over the leadership of the arts mission for the outgoing retiree. It was a test and trial of sorts, to see if my character would stand up and fit the role.

When I left New Zealand, I had no clue that this was behind the invitation to Kenya. I had simply responded to where I knew God was calling me, and as He led, I followed obediently. I had heard that the current missionary was planning to retire, but my family was in no stage of life to fulfill that type of role, nor was it a call I had felt personally. I had no desire to take this position up or commit to any mission agency. The problem was, the outgoing missionary felt God had told her to bring me, and she was certain that was His plan for inviting me.

In the meantime, another person had stepped into the role. She had spent a lot of effort to be there and was totally unaware of this hidden motive. No wonder there was warfare afoot! Thinking she already had the position, this woman was struck with jealousy when I arrived. An ugly spirit of competition arose and began manifesting in disturbing ways.

A very awkward discussion ensued, and as God showed me the insecurities of the people involved, I felt His compassion and was able to humble myself and see the situation turned around.

Thank God for the word of warning that had prepared me to discern the presence of this spiritual attack. As the days went on, I continued to seek heaven for the right strategies, just as Joshua had. I relied on the fact that God had a plan, and it would come to pass. Surely, He would not bring me this far for nothing! Trusting that everything would work out, I listened carefully to Holy Spirit's leading each day.

In one of my morning reflection times, God spoke to me from Job 42v1-2 (NCV):

> *"I know that you can do all things and that no plan of yours*
> *can be ruined."*

This verse strengthened me as I felt the Lord's encouragement that He certainly did have a definite plan and purpose for me to be there, and I should hold on to that as I waited upon Him to reveal everything in His good time. In the meantime, I decided to take in my surroundings and appreciate where I was, and how magnificent it was that I was even there.

Like Joshua, God would give me heavenly strategies to see the battle won and the walls of strife come down. God gives the power to win. But it wasn't only for me—this was my time to rise in leadership.

> *Then the Lord said to Joshua: "Don't be afraid; don't give up..."*
> *Joshua 8:1 (ERV)*

God called Joshua to be a strong and courageous leader, a person of influence with a deep love for his people, one who is victorious through obedience and faith.

God revealed it all and the truth surfaced during the final week of the mission.

The challenge all along had been unspoken agendas and a lack of clear communication. This gave rise to offense and bitterness, which in turn opened spiritual doors for the enemy to begin stirring the insecurities hidden within hearts.

How important it is not to get caught up in the agendas of others, no matter how much they dress it up in God-speak. I could see that the enemy was still very much out to steal, kill and destroy my destiny and would be on hand to try and snatch my inheritances as quickly as I began to walk in them, if I let him! But the condition of our heart when it is put under intense pressure is where the real battle is won.

As I prepared to leave Africa for home, God spoke to me once more through Joshua 10:8 (NCV):

> *"Don't be afraid of those armies, because I will hand them over to you. None of them will be able to stand against you."*

I took this promise for myself and stood up in what His Word said. On the last day of the residency, I read the account in Joshua 10 where he commands the sun to stand still. This was a miracle amongst the elements of the natural world, brought about at faith's request.

With one command, God took care of the opposition (mostly with hailstones!), leaving very little for Joshua's army to do for themselves.

Blessing my counterpart, I asked God to show her the areas that needed an increase of grace and power in her life, and prayed sincerely and compassionately that God would bring peace to her heart and help her settle her worth in Him.

I left Africa for home with a humbled heart, friendships and networks that have stood the test of time and proved themselves to be true God-connections, a restored love for missions, and a much greater understanding of the inheritance of leadership.

Upon returning home, I was informed, sadly, that the woman involved in the misunderstanding had not humbled her heart at all. She behaved viciously towards some of the national people we had been working with, and in the end, they refused to continue to work with her. Now she had been struck down with a terrible illness, and was unable to go into her next mission placement.

As it turned out, another person who was on the trip with me was appointed two years later to take over the mission. What an amazing outcome! I encourage you, whenever you can bring healing or blessing, do it. Even the most humbling of seasons brings out the best in us when we submit fully to being restored.

But there was one more lesson from the life of Joshua for me to embrace.

In Joshua 14, we see the process of allotment of the new lands to the people of God. In this account, Caleb comes to Joshua and reminds him of God's promise to him through Moses, to which Joshua was a witness. Caleb does this to ensure he won't miss out on his inheritance. From that time on, the land had rest from war (Joshua 14:13-15). There was peace in Hebron. Years earlier, Caleb brought a good report when everyone else brought a poor report, and he was rewarded well for it.

Upon reflection, the whole experience with the arts mission felt to me that I had been sent to Africa to 'spy out the land', but the real mission for me was yet ahead. However, my report had not been so good.

I came home from that trip and complained about how terrible things had been for me. In so doing, I almost missed how good it had been for God. I needed to learn to guard my mouth and keep my focus on what God is doing, not what I am doing.

I prayed intensely and repented of my selfishness, asking for forgiveness and help to function better in the world around me while not losing sight of heaven's perspective. In that moment, feeling like a total hot mess that I had completely missed it, Holy Spirit gave me clarity.

In conversation with a friend from Africa, she explained that in her culture, the word "Welcome" is spoken to those who fit in or belong. Suddenly I understood that the word I had heard so often was an expression of the peoples' embrace of me. Everywhere I had been in Africa, people kept saying welcome. Now I knew why!

I hadn't missed it at all. I had captured the hearts of the people for God.

Despite the spiritual battle I encountered, being in Africa had seemed natural and normal to me. I was not insensitive to the increasing hardships and poverty in the environment where the mission's work took place, but it was as if there was an ease to being there as well. It felt just like home; the people felt like home for me. I had a similar experience when I served in Cambodia and when I lived in Papua New Guinea—God gave me a heart love for both the land and its people. This is what it is to be part of God's eternal family; you simply belong! It's beyond earthly culture—it's *Kingdom*.

When we love people, they heal, and as they are healed, the land they inhabit is also healed through the love of God pouring out of us. This is how nations will be restored—through the love of God.

> *"Surely the land where your foot has trodden shall be your inheritance and your children's forever, because you have wholly followed the Lord my God"*
> Joshua 14:9

I went to Africa according to the Lord's will and now have a sense that there is a place for me in Africa always. I want to return one day with my whole family. Having learnt to speak of the goodness of God in the land of the living, I know our reward will be great.

In Joshua 15, Caleb's daughter, Aksah, is given in marriage to Othniel as a reward for subduing the occupiers of the land that had been allocated to Caleb. In turn, Caleb's daughter asks her father for a field of her own—and for springs of water as well. Even though she was getting married, it seems she wanted to secure her own inheritance.

Her father gives her all that she asks for!

Putting aside the astonishing miracle this is for the time and within this culture, this woman knew she could not let her inheritance go. Her husband may have *won* the land, but it was not enough; she wanted to be *given* a portion of the land promised through Moses from the Lord.

I thought about the lands where my feet had trodden, places where I had spiritual blessing and authority. I remembered the day I received a call from Cambodia to tell me that foundation stones were being laid for a new building. Because of my service to the people there, my name was to be placed on these stones. From Kenya I also received the request that my name be etched into the clay foundation of the arts school in Nairobi.

In both cases, I asked that Joshua 24:15 be written instead:

> *"Choose for yourselves this day whom you will serve . . . but as for me and my house, we will serve the Lord."*

This verse, which is displayed in my own home, is now written upon foundation stones in these two nations. Like the woman with the issue of blood, I reached out for more of God, and as a result, I have spiritual 'children' in the land—an inheritance among the nations.

I finish this book with a challenge to put your heart on the line for God.

To give up your life to follow Jesus, means to give up your alliances with pain, hurt, wounds and anger, and allow the love of the Father to break down the walls of defense you have built and cleanse your heart of the trappings of this world. It means letting Him restore the true *Kingdom Within* to how it was always meant to be.

I started this book by telling you that my entire life I have been a seeker of love. As I have grown and matured, I have become a seeker of faith and justice as well, both for myself and others. It has made me tired and weary at times, and in truth, this last season has tested me greatly and caused me to question some areas of my life even more. But the hope within me has remained, and I cannot shake it.

I choose to remain positive, despite the negative influences in the world around us. I refuse to give in to the darkness, and believe wholeheartedly that the light of the hope and glory of Christ who is alive in me will cause the gates of hell to not prevail in the lives of those I love and encounter.

We are being called to a time of increased faith (Matthew 21:22), blessing (Genesis 22:17), courage (Acts 4:29), authority (Luke 10:19), and favor (Acts 22:14). As we respond to that call we will see a manifestation of momentum, miracles and multiplication take place throughout our families, cities, and nations, just as in all the stories God has had me share with you through this book.

> *"The Spirit of the Lord God is upon Me, because the Lord has anointed Me to preach good tidings to the poor; He has sent Me to heal the brokenhearted, to proclaim liberty to the captives, and the opening of the prison to those who are bound"*
> Isaiah 61:1

As I release this book, I pray that your life will not only be impacted but transformed, and that you will be delivered into the fullness of the glory of God. God is raising dead hearts back to life! May your *Kingdom Within* begin to explode with new revelation and breakthrough.

I urge you also, have the courage and strength to share your story with others. Our stories and the messages we receive originate in the heart of God. When we write them, they are delivered from the glory realms to earth, from the highest heavens into the hands of all mankind. There truly are others out there just waiting to hear or read to encounter God for themselves through your story.

I encourage you to begin by praying. After all, "Prayer is just a conversation, so why don't you just have one?"

May God bless you as you walk out your story, the story of His Kingdom on earth, as it is in heaven.

All my love, Sharon

AN INVITATION

If this book has resonated with you in any way and you now feel ready for a life of transformation from the place you find yourself in today to the place you are designed and destined for, I invite you to pray this prayer with me:

God,

Today I turn my heart towards You. I acknowledge that Jesus Christ is Your Son and that He died on the Cross and rose again, overcoming death, so that I may live. I repent of my sins and ask for Your forgiveness. Renew in me a right spirit and create in me a clean heart, Lord, and fill me today with Your Holy Spirit. In Jesus' name, Amen

> *And he brought them out and said, "Sirs, what must I do to be saved?" So they said, "Believe on the Lord Jesus Christ, and you will be saved, you and your household." Then they spoke the word of the Lord to him and to all who were in his house. And he took them the same hour of the night and washed their stripes. And immediately he and all his family were baptized.*
> Acts 16:30-33

You are now a new creation and have been set free. I encourage you to find a local church or fellowship and become strengthened in your decision by being baptized with water as you follow Christ.

DECLARATION

I encourage you to take this declaration and make it a daily deposit into your life by faith until you see the manifestation of its utterances begin to come forth.

> *I have been forgiven and set free.*
>
> *I acknowledge that I have a past, but that past no longer defines me.*
>
> *I no longer walk in the shadow of lies and shame.*
>
> *I have already been forgiven and set free and am no longer a captive to anything or anyone.*
>
> *Just as I have and will do, my children have and will make mistakes, but they too are forgiven and set free from the captivity of any shame, historical or otherwise.*
>
> *We as a family are no longer bound by the accuser; we are forgiven and set free.*
>
> *I live in freedom.*
>
> *I walk in dignity and humility as a risen one and will keep moving forward in the liberty of a healed and free heart.*
>
> *I am no longer broken-hearted or bound but completely reconciled, restored, and free!*
>
> *In Jesus' name, Amen*

PROPHETIC WORD FOR THE AUTHOR

As I sat with Holy Spirit ready to send the final manuscript off to my editor and publisher, I received a prophetic word from a trusted prophetic artist and friend confirming that it was the right time to release this book, and that through it, captives would be set free to receive the fullness of the Kingdom of Glory.

He wrote:

"As I was praying for you, I saw Jesus with his sleeves rolled up, tossing aside his carpenter's tool belt. It appeared he was working on a house, a mansion. This house belongs to you. As he was building this home, he made sure there would be everything you needed. This home has many rooms. It could be likened to your heart. It would appear that he has finished the construction of this home and is now ready to get his bride. His horse is waiting for him right outside the house.

All this time Jesus has been working in your heart, he has been preparing the foundation of this home. There were times he had to tear down, and on rare occasions, to rebuild. He found that every beam, every stud, every window served as a purpose to shore up this house. He was there working when you were not sure of certain things that caused you to doubt. All your brokenness was spackled up, repainted, and made to look like nothing was ever broken. He had to dig up huge stones and rocks that were offsetting the foundation a little. He had to move the structure to get to it.

We hide specific issues in our hearts that God will not touch unless you allow him to. To remove those issues requires moving the structure and then rebuilding it again. But now it appears that he has completed his work. Oh, you're not perfect, and neither is any human being on the face of this earth. But you carry passion for the things of the Lord. He trusts you to complete the home with design and furniture. Hope, faith, and love are the components that will give beauty to this home. The house is ready, daughter of God."

ACKNOWLEDGMENTS

I want to acknowledge God first and foremost in all I do—He gets all the glory!—Jesus Christ as my Lord and Saviour, and Holy Spirit as my best friend.

To Craig Reynolds—my husband, my biggest supporter, and my greatest fan always. Thank you for your commitment to pick up your cross and love me daily.

To my children—Jessica, Catherine, Lydia, Daniel, Shaun and Amy. Thanks for being such cool kids!

To my mentor, Pastor Jennifer Eivaz for her continuing faith in who God is in me and her unfailing love and encouragement always.

To those who gave endorsements for this book, my ministry colleagues and friends—thank you for your support and desire to see Holy Spirit transform lives through my writings.

As always, without my friend & editor Anya McKee by my side throughout the birthing process, this book would not be in your hands today. I remain thankful for this divine connection, and that Anya continues to honour my voice being heard.

ABOUT THE AUTHOR

Whaea Sharon Reynolds leads The HIVE NZ Ltd., impacting nations with her innovative programs, ideas, expertise and leadership. She is a creative entrepreneur, an exhibited artist and accomplished writer, as well as wife, mother and grandmother. *Whaea* (pronounced 'fire') is an indigenous Māori title given to Sharon by her people as a leader and mother to the nations. Sharon is of Ngati Kahangunu and Te Arawa descent.

Whaea Sharon's work has taken her into the high schools and prisons of Aotearoa and Africa, and into Cambodia where she has worked with children rescued from trafficking. Her unique programs and workshops use mixed modalities that offer hope. She works to bring justice to those who live with injustice, and to see people and communities transformed by the love and redeeming power of Christ.

To find out more or connect with Sharon, please visit:
www.thehivenz.org

ALSO BY SHARON REYNOLDS

Available at www.thehive.org
or through online retailers

www.ingramcontent.com/pod-product-compliance
Lightning Source LLC
LaVergne TN
LVHW011725060526
838200LV00051B/3034